Praise for Linda Bamber's *Metropolitan Tang*

Urbane and heartbroken, Linda Bamber's voice is wonderfully fresh and original, and the substance of her poems, for all their playfulness of style, deeply serious and humane. She belongs to an improvisatory tradition, so as readers we feel the surprise and integrity of the method in the spontaneity and organic discoveries of the poem.

As a reader I have often wished, over the years, for a female poet in the style of [Frank] O'Hara: bopping but sincere, humanistic and grounded but exuberant and irreverent. Linda Bamber may be that person.

TONY HOAGLAND

Linda Bamber's poems are edgy, aware, urgent and dazzling. I love their sudden shifts and disruptive methods—her insistence on connections most of us would like to deny. There are dark truths here, expressed with wit and feeling . . . a first-rate book.   KATHA POLLITT

Linda Bamber's poems offer the deepest of pleasures. Often funny, and alert to the intricacies and surprising, eruptive energy of colloquial speech, this work deftly and vividly mixes the quotidian with the histori- cal, literary, religious and philosophical.   LAURIE SHECK

The interplay between sophisticated irony and candid emotional vulnera- bility gives Linda Bamber's poetry its characteristic charming truthful- ness. Bamber never pretends not to know she's writing a poem, but at the same time she often gives the feeling that she's talking with us over a glass of wine. I love the many surprises presented by her work.

MARK HALLIDAY

Metropolitan Tang

poems

Linda Bamber

A Black Sparrow Book
David R. Godine · *Publisher*
Boston

For my sister Patsy

This is
A Black Sparrow Book
published in 2008 by
David R. Godine, Publisher
Post Office Box 450
Jaffrey, New Hampshire 03452
www.blacksparrowbooks.com

The Black Sparrow Books pressmark is by Julian Waters
www.waterslettering.com

LIBRARY OF CONGRESS CATALOGING-IN-PUBLICATION DATA
Bamber, Linda.
Metropolitan tang / by Linda Bamber.
p.   cm.
Poems.
ISBN-13: 978-1-57423-213-4
ISBN-10: 1-57423-213-4
I. Title.
PS3602.A6345M47   2008
811'.6—dc22
2007047854

First Edition
PRINTED IN CANADA

CONTENTS

Thought's mid,
telegraphic form a mobile

routine!

less interesting

Familiarity

Teenagers for sure, one black, one white,
so when did they have that terrified, high-pigtailed
child? in yellow and pink,

screaming *Mommy, Mommy,*
at Sherman and Walden as I bike through.
The boy stands in the street, you'd say

irresolute, but his (good-looking) face is calm.
As if I were the child I see the mother's violent face
and then her back. *I won't take care of you,*

she shouts, and points to him and storms away.
Every bone in the child's body breaks from being dropped
or rather hurled, a clattering breakage of plates in flight.

I don't know you, man, says the boy from the street,
but doesn't leave, at least. I'm stupefied, straddling my bike
in glasses and mirror-rigged helmet, all this useless

apparatus on my head for seeing
and not getting hurt. Everything that happens
all her life may have to pass through this

cool May 6 P.M., the dandelions in the sidewalk cracks,
the hardware store, the parking lot,
the biker like a staring bug.

Well, that's a woman's weapon, no?
Smash the thing you're known to care about;
rip the shirt you made yourself,

sob in front of guests.
It's over, asshole. You *pick up the pieces.*
Cry angrily while biking.

Will that show God (who made spring leaves)
how bitterly you disapprove
of his or her arrangements?

Essay on Art

The way you can tense up around art sometimes
like self-consciousness in bed

The way I totally missed
the confluence of three of the greatest artists of the last half century,
although I was there in Row P to see it:
the relentlessly sad
but apparently beautiful performance of
"Die Winterreisse" I might as well have been
channel surfing as gone to Jordan Hall to hear.
The man who got it. I saw him wait before he clapped,
I saw his face, I saw it all go into his body
rearranging him
before the cheering started.

The way the drummer whipped his head
so fast you couldn't tell if he was looking at
the side he was striking or
the side he'd strike next. The way he
would suddenly stop
doing that with his head, face forward and grin
while his hands kept it up on the drum;
so we knew how unnecessary all that
head-whipping had been.

The way my father would look at a painting
until it was over and done; while I,
on the other hand,
drift back from other rooms
to look again.

The way the dancer said,
You never know if you'll make it that night;
and the soprano: will she hit the note? so we can explode.
We want our performers out on the edge
where only God can help them now.

The way a poem ends sometimes by changing;
and how Wang Wei and others
give bitterness short shrift.
For 13 years
I was at court; now, in exile, I . . .
whatever. How good it is to see them
roll things up regretlessly,
whole lives.
The way they asked the roshi
what he thought of Beethoven or Brahms.
The roshi thought a bit. After a silence,

Not enough silence, he said.

Beginning

Some men

you give them a little wine, a little sex
a little critique of their most
basic personality issues and also
of the pornographically photographed sailboat
they currently think would vault them,
if they owned it,
to a whole new level of happiness

(which it wouldn't, not with that lopsided
helm)

and they're done. They bury their head in your midriff
crying,
"I know you! I know what a pain in the neck you are!"

Is there anything not to like about men like that?
Exactly what?
Tell me, because I don't see it.

Yes

for Liz

Yes, I had fun in New York.
On the subway a woman was on about broccoli,
which was good for her cataracts and she was
writing a book about it, and she was still talking as I left
the nearly empty subway,
saying, "Broccoli, then," amused, and waggling my hand
goodbye. She went on talking as the doors closed,
correcting or amending something she had said,
some impression she had left that wasn't right
as the train pulled off;
and I made my way up
to the street

where it was 64 degrees in January
and the huge, complicated, unlovely
intersection smelled delicious
because it was lunchtime
and not everyone has my compunctions about eating
hot dogs and pretzels from carts.
The place was swarming with strangers (to me),
healthy, alive, eating delicious-smelling pizza with two or three friends
one knee up and foot against the wall
of a bank or a fly-by-night appliance
store. I found your building
easily enough, and we stood by the window
and talked.
As you know, that didn't go so well;

but as we talked we watched
Day 90 of a forty-story building being built,

the men working singly or in clumps
random motion as it seemed
but united by some Vision, maybe God's.
You kept binoculars to verify details;
I preferred the way the distance made all odds
even, the hammering, hoisting,
shifting, welding, moving, smiting
all going on at once.
Brief vehemence of gesture over here;
handshake seconds later over
                                        there.
"Guys," I heard someone call through the din.
"Doesn't fucking work! D. F. W.!"
At that I tried to catch your eye but failed.
Someone completed a task and twirled
his tool to celebrate; only I
saw the tiny hammer
spin. From your place I went to the

museum. Upstairs the art was
short white lengths of string on bright black
floor, resembling
unsteady speech. All of a sudden I was
exhausted, which is what happens in New York sometimes;
it wasn't seeing you that
did me in. That night
I saw Saturn plain
through a scope near the Time Warner building.
At first all I saw
was blackness in the eyepiece, but then something jumped
in and out, catching me quite off guard.
This was

the Real! A silent, matte white
sphere with tilted rings
indifferent, absolute. It seemed an ancestor, long dead
and yet alive
moving from room to room
or putting on a coat, beyond indifferent to
the gawkers looking back. There was no way to play with it,
compete or condescend. How had I
forgotten it, or never
thought to look?
People came out of the stores

cosmetic stores, clothing stores with shiny windows
polished lit and clean. Cold black night, bright light stores
high atrium with huge bronze statues
mimicking soft flesh. I saw this building go up,
too; but all things pass, and so will this;
and so will you. In fact,
I've already erased
the message you left on my machine
asking if I had fun in New York.
This is to tell you
yes, I did,
although it seems strange of you to ask
as if you had nothing to do with it.

Metropolitan Tang

Across the street
in the green-signed Alamo/National lot
a Greek Orthodox priest has just exchanged his high black
hat for a close-fitting beanie;
hugged a man in a purple parka
and driven off in sunglasses
flowing beard and robes.

I like that!
I like living someplace
people come!
bringing their beliefs.

Where do you live? I asked the robed and bibbed Zen monk
(and vet)
last week
Nowhere, he said,
and out came such a story
his wanderings, begging for food;
Vietnam;
how he had killed so many men
at two hundred he lost track.
Out, too, came his anger, not yet burned clean
but silenced every quarter hour by a bell
rung by his assistant
with such precision as to how and when she prayed
you'd think a cutting tool'd been used.
The burning monk would stop each time;
a murderer, transformed;
and his assistant, by the way, a German girl
from Schleswig-Holstein
immaculate in robe and bib and pantaloons

with turquoise plastic frames
on her glasses. I like

the Asian students' laptops in my Starbucks
their screens displaying characters
like scattered straw;
and someone teaching someone
Turkish right close by. Everyone's
from somewhere else
or on our way to where we never started from.
From Samarkand

musicians make their way to town
riding a Tang
dynasty camel.
Four just sit with instruments, but one

in a loose green shirt that nevertheless reveals
a slight, soft midriff bulge
stands
up leaning
towards Xian
as if the Silk Road desert crossing
hasn't laid a glove on him. The camel, too,
feels fine, his head erect, his feet foursquare.
The city teems with traders,
vendors, customs, costumes,
languages
and multicultural food.
Manicheans, Zoroastrians, and Nestorian
Christians! Bring on
the musicians! But who are they

exactly? Why didn't I get
an audio guide?
I eye the fellow next to me
who did—
hopefully at first, but soon
expectantly; and then (if truth be told)
impatiently. I'm a piece of work, I guess! But

whatever movie I'm in,
he's in, too, because he nods
and takes his headset off
to tell me what he's heard. *Yes,*
he says, *it's great;* acknowledging my right
as if he were my father,
husband, son. He tells me
this and that
and we pause a moment there—
he and I and this
three-colored
drip-glazed work

the gorgeous cloth beneath the saddle hanging
dripping
down.

not the
best ending

17

Sound System

I hate concerts
The whole concept of the intermission makes me sick
When the soloist says something endearing and waves of warm feelings
ripple up to the balcony
hit the back wall and return
I feel hideously taken advantage of

But to be in
the traffic and parking of everyday life
the ATM's and the BBC's, no,
to have turned off the BBC and put in a CD instead
to drive my irritating stoplighted route
the sky sour and the storefronts dour

while Claudio Arrau does something to the piano that climbs
to a mountaintop
and there unleashes wild extreme and world-commanding gestures
of emotional self-assertion

and it is ME up there, repeating flinging commanding
among the edelweiss
while a helicopter circles and gets it all on camera

is like wearing scarlet underpants.

Academic in Traffic

Whether the language rebellion against phallogocentrism is really
the deepest thing or
just a way of getting out of history
i.e., race, class and gender, so
tiresome, so unavoidable; whether, that is, poetry, etc.,
no matter how weird, surreal, anti-referential, disruptive, etc.,
accepts things as they are when they need to be changed?
What are we doing, we who tend words?
Who read signs? Who read?
Overhead a billboard moans

exhausted inspiration.
"When a man's mind has been stretched by a new idea,"
it says,
then blah and blahdy blah.
It supervises cars that writhe and buck
below
till anarchists, enraged, invade it.
"When a man's anus has been stretched by a big penis . . ."
they make it say,

and my brother, double-taking,
sees a mother covering
her children's eyes. Some
language intervention, huh?
And yet that's not our way.
Is it anything to wait, in an agony of inactivity,
for language to arrive? To be there when it does?
What shall I tell my students?
Whatever I say they will part believe, part writhe under;
then they'll whirl off to their lives
like leaves; their historical lives.

Bulls

for Frieda, and in memory of Grace

To speak of women's friendships is boring
it is tiresome
I am bored already, just broaching the topic . . .

Having attained the summit
which turned out to be a meadow
with benches
we sat and talked. There were some cows in a
clump.

The best writer living in America today
may well be a woman; but she won't be that
much longer, because, you told me then,
she's dying.

I do not want her to go.

It was humid, and the fabled
five-town view obscure in haze.
The cows turned out to be young bulls
so close they almost touched. I touched the

famous woman writer once.
In fact, my arm around her back,
I love you, G., I said.
Thank you, Linda, she replied in all
simplicity; although it was hellishly hot
and the place was full of her

adoring fans. Of course, I love you, too, my dear.
The bulls abruptly changed position
like a cloud of gnats
on the diagonal
together. You're an activist,
like G. My long view
distresses you. We couldn't think
of anything new
to say about women's friendships
though G. took a stab once; not her best
story, too bad. The bulls were horsing

and shoving around.
One wrenched his head back, throwing a shower
of half-chewed grass
intensely green
on his black back—
as Jove, a bull once himself,
once showered bright gold on a girl.
Just mad at the flies, I said; but it seemed
like a new twist
or maybe the start of a whole new myth.
I'll see you once in town

before you go.
Winter will be cold and dark again
in both our cities; dark and long. What if the winter stars
flung like the grass over night's black back
are really friends and fans of G.?—
gathered now to hear her read

some new, successful,
soon-to-be-classic story on women's friendships.
When winter comes, we could look up.
Look up, sweetheart, some winter night.
Find some bright star and make it G.; and think of me.

(2006)

Whether This Marriage Is Ending

Some Thoughts on Watching Eyes on the Prize
with the New Freshman Class

Whether the privileging of the pastoral tradition in Afro-American
      women's writing is bad for "the urban confrontation of
      race, class, and sexuality"

Whether we should pay the house taxes out of the joint account
Whether I should be writing this or something else

Whether I am really interested in state formation in the early
      modern period
Or should just teach *Richard II* out of "Notes on 'Camp,'" as planned
Whether it isn't better, after all, to have fewer feelings
      and get more done

Whether there was something I could have done to keep
      Martin Luther King from being assassinated
and the movement alive

Whether our students understand that segregation, although filmed in
      black and white, was
yesterday, and those girls in crinolines going up the school steps are
      alive, and still not even all that old

Whether it matters if they do

Whether the satisfaction of our material needs makes all this inner
      turmoil inevitable, for we are, as Primo Levi said,
a stack of needs

which makes George Herbert right as well
in "The Pulley"

and Frieda and Jon also right, particularly Frieda
who sees female lamentation as part of the romance of war

Whether my tears just keep the economy humming

Whether the whole house has to come down, roof siding framing gutters
        side porch front porch staircase floors

and the bushes we planted along the foundations,
leaving only
a hole in the ground

Whether to sink into it or snap out of it—

What to do with my day.

All Mixed Up

Who's to blame
Who's to blame for blaming

Forgetting what I specifically asked you to do
Being late all the time

Not being willing to talk about it
Turning it against me when I do.

Drinking too much.
Trying to control me!

Walking away from me on holiday
sitting on the ruined wall,
thinking of leaving
as evening fell.

Leaving? What are you *talking* about?
I can't believe you're leaving me!
I'm not leaving you!
Don't leave me!
You don't quit, you're fired!

Don't you take so much as one CD.
Here, take the picture of us
at your grandmother's that time; and
don't you want the album I made you
for your birthday?

Documents aside,
they would always be married.
They aren't married any more.

Do you remember
the grandmotherly blue hydrangeas
by the porch? Fine, then,
neither do I!

I'm going now, goodbye.

I don't think about you any more.

Drinking too much . . .
Forgetting what I specifically asked you to do . . .

Suddenly the City

I live in seems interesting
as if I were on vacation here
and feeling indulgent
towards the human race, its way of
living in cities and
tearing up roads so the traffic has to be
re-routed around a collapsing white mesh barrier
as in this intersection here.
The people of this city
walking back and forth on the sidewalks
each one having gotten up and dressed this morning
look like this, this
movie, almost, of people crossing the street.
The questions,
is this scene in any way rewarding to look at?
e.g., architecturally, in terms of city spaces and human interest; and
are things diverse enough here? and
are these people, in general,
older or younger than I am? just now are
in abeyance. In their absence is this
pleasant sense that there are many cities in the world
and this is one of them.
It rained earlier. I think I'll go see the monks
make a sand mandala on the Esplanade; and
who knows, later I might get a sandwich.

Two Epiphanies (Connected by the Word "Then")

Gloomy, mortal, angry,
    you lie on the beach, dune-backed,
staring at waves
        some distance out.

"Go ahead," you've said to your companion.
        He walks down the beach
        while you sit, not seeing
                        much.

No, you sit in traffic, stuck
in thoughts starring you,
        an unpleasant, unsuccessful person;
        near a little scene between
        a Chinese woman and a child.

They're dressed and ready to leave the house
but each time she grabs him down
        from the sill
        he climbs back up. Noticing

her salt-and-pepper hair, *No spring chicken,*
you think—just like you. It's when the tiny
        child gets down himself,

—the left knee squat
        the cautious foot—

that you know you have been watching, after all,
and so has she, neither knowing what
        was going on.
The child had to do it himself

or die on the doorstep: no,
he *wouldn't* let his grandma get him down.

When you see the woman's face
break up in sudden-understanding laughter

      just a flash, because
they're turning down the street—

      you and she
(although she doesn't know you're there)
one sudden-understanding thing—

then ocean waves throw seabirds up
before their foam

and your companion
walking further down the beach
      is suddenly, unknowingly absolved.

Did I mention those
      wave-born
            black specks?
I didn't even know I'd
noticed them
or wondered what they were.

I tell you, they were birds!

Venice

Venice flooded
only 6 3 K people living there now
tourists by the millions daily, gone by night
people wading in boots, bare feet
St. Mark's flooded
the front steps along the canals visible only
at low water
brilliant green with algae

the earth sinking, the sea rising
the politicians promising
the floodgates designed tested perfected
but not built. The vegetable market
going on anyway; plywood, planks over water,
lines of people going both ways on makeshift boardwalks
congested, narrow. Life goes on. The people move

upstairs, lean out flower-boxed windows
on canals. Water seeps, spreads; silent. Some cities,

says Simon Winchester
are where they should be, London, Paris,
not Pompeii. Some day we'll visit abandoned
San Francisco, see the stumps of the
Golden Gate Bridge. Petra,
Herculaneum, goodbye. But

unthinkable lose Venice
where is NATO or the National Guard?
This is Venice, so special, so famous,

not my favorite
Italian city, so what? I don't like to lose things
not Venice, not anyone I've ever
loved
at all, not my poem-worthy thoughts
not one . . .

Shoreline views
slipping by
can I catch and put them in a poem?

fall day
train running on schedule
egrets and ospreys slipping by
swans, mallards, herons
sweeping phragmites, bad invasive; biodiversity
slipping by
so, as Bob says, should we all just kill ourselves?

boatyards with big white plastic
shrink-wrapped boats
evocative towns

highways alongside now
green signs overhead
New Haven in the right place or doomed?
New London will I ever catch the ferry
as I mean to
visit my friend Jon?
People at the reunion last week

their lives slipping by
mostly lawyers; old
babes with yearbook pictures of themselves
around their necks

good looks definitely going

    son's difficulties okay now meds adjusted

    never thought I'd make pots all my life but
that's what I do

    still wildly in love with my husband

room dense with stories, lives, lies
Americans all
get a second chance.

Yet

cities rise and fall
one and all. New York
will you be there when the train gets in?
Towers? Flowers
sold from sidewalk buckets?
Steps to the Met
ascending to art?
It would really be a bummer if you weren't.
It would seriously fuck

with my plans.

Homage to Frank O'Hara

I wake up too early, read for a while.

Thich Nhat Hanh says not to mind having one's spiritual quest
interrupted by one's life
but just to be mindful and
not get impatient if someone is talking to you.

No one is talking to me. It's 5 A.M.

The notion that sleeping is something natural, says Marcel Mauss,
is completely inexact. I read this in an essay connecting
ethnography to surrealism where it is meant to be outrageous
but to me it's merely accurate. I stopped sleeping
naturally in Paris
when I was six. When Mauss was in

Paris in the early twenties there were manifestos
and movements, mostly of men. At one
famous banquet, says the essay,
*Phillippe Soupault swings from a chandelier, kicking over bottles
        and glasses*
which is intellectual history for you if you
tell the story often enough.

In Paris I couldn't sleep,
didn't like the water,
gagged on garbage day.
Thich Nhat Hanh says we should stay where we are
not be in such a hurry to get on with things;
and above all we should know
whether or not we have moved away from our breath.

Once you have reached
such an awareness
there will be nothing you need fear anymore.

This isn't meant to sound outrageous.

I believe him.

Comforted
as I was not comforted in Paris
by reading when the others were asleep
about Lexington and Concord in a children's book
but as I *was* comforted last week in Santa Fe
by reading about Marcel Mauss
after which I fell asleep

I fall asleep. When I wake up I disapprove of myself
for knowing the intimate details of too many people's lives.
Errands, phone calls, chores; then Frank O'Hara,
sometimes hard to understand.
Can't understand Rimbaud at all,
wrote Joseph Conrad. *Wish you would come and shoot me.*

O'Hara
had lots of friends
and was always reading something choice.
His bed floated on a sea of books
into which
he trailed his hand when he woke up

for something to stay conscious for.
Thich Nhat Hanh says we should dedicate one day a week

at least to consciousness, posting perhaps a sign
above our beds the night before
reminding us that

this is it.
Do not depart, he urges.
This homeland is as beautiful as the homeland of your childhood.
My mother calls
but I offend her.
My uncle died last week,

my father long ago.
The other thing about O'
Hara is
his life can seem as pointless
sometimes
as my own. Art, friends, walks—

that's it. I fall asleep.
Art, friends, walks, naps. And now
for a touch of ethnographic surrealism
right here in Massachusetts
I shave my legs
because I'm going to a party and it's hot.

This is not the kind of party where intellectual history is made and a
"melee erupts between the surrealists and conservative patriots."
This is the first office party of a software company
funded by Fred's group, and
I'm there as his wife in a summer skirt. Can you imagine
Frank O'Hara, Joseph Conrad, Marcel Mauss, and Thich Nhat Hanh

shaving their legs for such an event? The people at the party
      are so smart
even the music is good. Altogether
(ripe pineapple, clean rugs, huge screen PCs)
the place is bursting with talent. *May you have fun*
getting rich
with integrity

as the poster said last week in Santa Fe. There was a number
      you could call
to learn how.
I listen to the Schubert
and also to the noises Stoney Ballard has on his machine.
When you throw away text you hear dogs
barking, bits of tunes, a woman at the climax

of love. It's very funny,
really. In 1925 in Paris *Michel Leiris is soon at an open window,*
      denouncing
France to the growing crowd
but here in the suburbs of Boston
the room is closed against the heat. In Paris I
stood at the bottom of a street of stairs, my father

in his great role as
my father. *From here,*
I tentatively said,
it almost seems as if the clouds can move. Paris
was gray, architectural, proportioned, façaded, stairwayed.
Loose enormous clouds rushed by: how could that be?

My father only said they can and do; but that
changed everything. It was
my father, then,
who made clouds move
converting at a stroke the unreal city
into the homeland of my childhood

swept like the veldt with motion overhead.
He was younger than I am now by as many years as I was
old
then.

It was easier to love a homeland
that had him in it,
that's for goddamn sure.

Donne's the One

It wasn't cool to like those school assemblies
but I did
hundreds of us in beat-up brown wooden
seats, someone stumbling
through "Death Be Not Proud," all of us singing
some dumb song. I liked the film about menstruation
focusing on the pituitary gland;

the incompetent dances and plays.
I liked the address to us all—
not just my friends, but
kids who were Different, too, off-limits kids whose eyes
we avoided, and then just
row upon row of others
we didn't even know.
There was no effort in it. When they told us to stand
we just stood.
We said the Gettysburg Address
if we could.

Last night I dreamed some similar
scene . . .
not an auditorium
an armory, perhaps;
somewhere people shelter in
emergencies

try to get their kids to sleep
on blankets on the floor.
A speaker was asking us questions
while we gazed at him

from molded orange chairs.
How many, he asked,
knew someone with AIDS?
Or anything! A girl
perhaps, afraid to fall asleep
in case she dreams again
about her weight; or someone here
in exile
from his now nonexistent native land?
(Countries do
come to an end, you know.)
Think of it, urged the speaker.
Living in stage sets, the people around him mere
puppets and ghosts!
Soon (of course)
we all had stood. *All whom the*
flood did and the fire shall o'erthrow,
All whom war, dearth, age, agues, tyrannies,
Despair, law, chance hath slain—all of us
had stood, and for ourselves
not someone else. Now we could meet
each other's eyes. The others felt in varying degrees
relief.
We all felt that;
plus joy.

Greeting

It's bad enough you've been away a week;
did you have to
be so late tonight and also
wake me up when you got back?
Pushing the door that sticks
until it loudly cracked
KSHBNK! Pissed, I thought I'd

just not move; feign sleep;
but then I changed my mind,
I guess.

You came . . .

not looping, like a sideways snake
making a show of elegant
unhurriedness
while getting off the road
with all due speed
for all of that;

nor like the beach grass tips
the breeze with little touches
hints and ruffles into waves;

like nothing but
the prompt, smooth muscles of a man
when arms he wants to be in
reach out to him in bed. You could have been
a robber. I had my eye mask on.
We slept blind, without a word.

Chinese Poet

Readings, ambitions,
         the struggle
    to listen

World-weary
poets;
    all of our issues.

But now here's a
        voice
    from far away:

flute notes floating
      through all interception.
Now the tax collection's

done at last. Rain, my books . . .
      the peace in this province
    is not to my credit, I guess.

Over his words
      like a leaf
   unease.

Relief! A breath,
     a ray; o poem
   with nothing to say.

Ecological Tourism

We are led by great commanders.
"Bolivar, Bolivar, Bolivar, me copias?"
says Napoleon
into his communications device.
Cheek to cheek we sit in the *panga*
our flotation devices orange,
our sunblock 30-plus.
Panga to *panga* they communicate.
We are:
a manager a counselor an investor a
professor a hairdresser
an ophthalmologist an archaeologist
an ex-anesthesiologist;
a grandmother of twelve and
a mother on the verge of grandness
waiting for an only chick.
"Bolivar, Bolivar, Bolivar, me copias?"
When we see a booby chick,
naked or overdressed
in tropical Polartec,
we click. Sony Sanyo Canon
Nikon Kodak Kodak Kodak Kodak click!
The intercom wakes us at six.
The precision of our operations
bears no relation to the tortoises
who've got all day to eat and mate.
At five we re-embark. Our leaders look nineteen.
"Bolivar, Bolivar, Bolivar, me copias?"
It is humbling
(if expensive)
to be a soldier in this army.

Nothing Evolves But Everything Certainly Changes

for my sister

First I refused to take pictures,
then I took pictures galore.
On the boat everyone was reading *Galápagos*
by Vonnegut, as surely would
the group that followed us
next week. Later:
a crater lake with orchids. Oh, everything reminded me delightfully
of someplace else!

All that beauty made me think of death
and once on a mountaintop, you,
who'd have loved it all:
how your not being there would
also be the case when you were dead—
although you're not—thank God, you're not—
which nailed me to the cloud-surrounded spot.

America del Sud! A world emerged from the mist
where fabulous things reside; as if it were an unknown thought
or its own off-shore islands, which come
and go in measurable time. Here animals arrive
by air or sea or seaweed raft
and vary and select. Here Darwin had
a fabulous idea.

I see I've said "here"
when I mean "there." I'm back in town
although I can't think why.
Have I told you how the Sally Lightfoot crab
gets up on points and runs? Have I told you that its chin

is *blue*? The drab, confusing finches were so
interesting, too! *These* (finch-related) *facts,*
as Darwin said, *undermine*

the stability of species.
And time and place and Self,
he might have said, and all facts, not just these.
In that case,

why stay home?
Hurry, hurry, come
see this bird point its beak at the sky
and widen its wings in love!
Sit in the sky and think of someone absent
you inordinately love. Why not?
The thought itself of death streams on,
as does the DNA.

Penelope

Ulysses came home, and things got better. 7 *nice launch*
The reunions, the recognitions,
all that was great, and great to get rid of those
loathsome

oafs. In the early years
I used to hang with them, eat their charred beef
(or rather, mine, or his).
I won't deny things sometimes went too far.
But either they got worse or I woke up
one day;
and then I just wanted them out.

He threw them out. Hurray.
I didn't mind
the blood. So if there's a sense of nostalgia or loss
I guess you can feel it for anything
past. It isn't the focus I miss,
the one thought, true north,

Ulysses, Ulysses, come home; mind like
a lighthouse sweeping the sea all night
with my wish. No;
what I miss is unweaving the shroud
and leaving no trace
of myself.
The visits from the gods,
the crying of my son, weave, unweave

divisionless, ahead of God.
My loneliness. The coming and
going of hope. The days closed up like water

45

when a ship's gone by. It felt so good one night
I went to where they kept the new-jarred wine
and spilled it in the dirt.

Now that life's gone
I'm queen again, which is to say
time's slave. I love

holding him at night, but even that
needs witnesses. From bed I listen to the moonlit sea.
It sees us, but it's not enough.

Hephaestus

The stars are scattered in the sky
irrespective of our need
for swans and lyres and charioteers.
Our dreams are foolish
and our constellations
fictions

that wouldn't fool a child. We teach them anyhow
as if God were a coloring book
as if, like the blacksmith god,
we thought to catch Love
in a net.

Fourth of July and Just After

for Bob

A flock of birds divides,
                reforms, inbreath
        and outbreath like a relaxing
sigh. All afternoon
the well-shaped clouds go by
              calm warriors
        emerging from the hills.
A heron shoots a long curved stream of white
        down through the air. At night

fireworks
        explode and float in orange strings
like a fine, fading beaded curtain
           fading and falling sideways
                  slower than their smoke.
           Is the city sliding slowly

to the right or the sky moving left?
        No matter. Orderly, satisfied,
the people stream home by the thousands.
        Midsummer midnight. Now
in the morning

comes
the unalarming whine
of the plumbing,
           winding down
                after being taxed.

Hairdresser Near Harvard Square

My hair is turning gray, gray
and needs to be turned back black.
It's a gray day, too; butt end of winter,
nothing but work.

Michael, though, turns my whole head bright
and offers ideas for my poem.
"Silver petals," he breathes overhead.
(It's a "foil process.") Then he

bends one knee and sprays the air
so I'll have hairspray smell as well.
Michael himself has shining locks
like a beautiful Regency fop;

blue jeans; great politics. Oh my
God, and a pierced tongue, which he
sticks out at me to explain
why he can't pronounce "Muffs" or "Moffs"

which I think is a band
he thinks I'll like because it's from
my time. Now my hair
is cooking;

the girls I'm sitting near compare
their answers on
the Ec exam. Was
"a random walk through the

consumption function," for instance,
right? They're coloring their hair for fun,

being young. I'm just glad this
foil process came in time

for this here-nor-there
stretch between my
real-colored hair and *oh-forget-it*.
"Forget it," says Michael to me

in the mirror,
pulling off the foil.
His father died last month; plus his uncle
and an aunt; next week he's

going under general for his knee.
"If I croak, I croak," he cries,
sweeping an arm, so I laugh. But
"I mean it," he says in the mirror

where he and I, in a dead season,
meet. As I drive home
some lights come on.
At least I've done my hair.

At least the pavement's bare
of ice; late March, the onion grass
will soon be up across the way.
It's six o'clock and not yet dark.

Just gray.

Conversations with the Sun

Sun, I said,
still thinking of Frank O'Hara,
who was thinking of Mayakovsky,
Stay there. No need to go away again this year.
It
was coming down like a man
from a crane, slow and careful not to swing
but then
attracted by the earth into a swift plumb
drop behind the hills—
which were already tonal
shapes as in a silkscreen print.
Last year the darkness

had gone inside my mind
and now I was afraid.
Do not, I said
with false authority
go off down Braintree Ridge—
gesturing
like King Canute.
The silence of the sun got more pronounced.

It held itself in tight
so not one least pink ray escaped.
Okay, I said (I got the point)
—goodbye; and blew my nose. Behind the hill it went,
catching a silo high on the slope
which shone as if it were

a multiprismed lighthouse lens.
Have you ever seen a Fresnel lens up

close? Great big glass things,
compound, complex,
like a periodic sentence, or a damselfly's eye.
Wild light flared forth:
aluminum reflections
for a few
precious seconds.

The sun reached up and grabbed
the light—

then nothing bright remained.

2. JUNG: NEW MEXICO

I think I'll climb a ladder
to the *kiva* roof
and watch, like Jung's Pueblo Indians,
the passage of the sun.

They wouldn't say
what secret filled the clear thin air:
grown men shaking with emotion
when the conversation touched
their religion. *Everyone can see*, said one,

the sun is God.
Without their prayers, the Pueblo said,
darkness would be at most

ten years away. Therefore they prayed
on the *kiva*.

Out of sheer envy, comments Jung,
we are obliged to smile at the Indians' naiveté;
to plume ourselves on our cleverness;
for otherwise we would discover
how down at heels we are.

Crabapple

The crabapples are covered now, flowers down each branch
like a long lumpy sock. Thick, elaborate frills: a
lamb chop bone the chef has taken trouble with. All over town
in chain-link yards with plaster

madonnas, by renovated
old New England houses where beetles eat
the ten-inch beams. The suburbs, of course. And beyond,
outside fake stores in mini-malls, the crabapples fewer

but not the number of flowers per overloaded tree;
pink hearts,
pink heat pushing out. Parking lots. And then
where things dribble off, not into country now but that
distressing mess we've got for in-between, helpless

with trafficky towns—crabapples, all the way out.
They came up from Georgia like notes on a chromatic
scale. Virginia, New York, we could hear them from here.
Now they're all on key

like a town whose church bells sound all
at once. Then—

quitting time. The choir stands
to leave the stage, black pants and skirts,
white shirts and blouses don't delay but go.
That's it. The blossoms make a light brown crust
like egg whites whipped and baked. The tree

is quite embarrassed now. It has opened its mouth
as if it had something
of great significance to say
and then in some embarrassment

didn't.

In the Tropics

The palm frond comes out rolled and sharp
as if it fought its way through flesh, not air.
I dislike its air of self-conscious
sincerity, its lack of self-knowledge,
its sense of being an example to the other
(bending, browning) fronds
and the whole scarred stem. Its sky-most extremity wobbles
like the lower lip of a schoolboy unjustly accused.
It thinks of England, and straightens its green,
too-ridiculous spine.

Cormorant

There's something wrong with me, says the black
                    cormorant, my
          body is too heavy or
something, even at rest I don't float
                    like other water birds, I
half-sink. I don't look right, I

know that. I'm not actually
                    sinking, but why don't I
          float, why does my neck
stick up at an angle?
                    There's something
wrong with me.

"When we loop around this way," shouts Jay
                    Segal, "there's a headwind
          going out and coming back."
Fine, I sarcastically think
                    and bike behind him like a bird
so he can break the wind. More shouting:

"Does that help?" Answer: No.
                    Why not?
          It helps other people but doesn't help
me. Pedal pedal too damn
                    much wind too hard. An
avocet runs right in front and all around

birds land and dive. Not that you could call it Nature here:
                    landfill with a narrow cinder path;
          naked industry across the bay.

On the other hand there are these
                    birds, some duck's lifted
terra-cotta tail, egg-yolk eyeliner

long curved beak.
                        If only
              they or I or the wind
would stop! Maybe there's a lesson
                    in the movement of the swift:
sinking and fighting forward, sinking and fighting

up. "It's a tough life," I puff in sympathy.
                              This
                    irritates the bird.
Working the wind the swift repeats,
                    "There's nothing wrong with me.
It says in the book I *sail between spurts,*

not all the livelong day."
                              So true!
              But wait: is this bravura on its part
or self-acceptance?
                    Look in the book
to see what it says about (pedaling

pedaling) me. "Sometimes it takes this type
of person months
to know
an outing wasn't fun."

Elizabeth Bishop on Brattle Street

When she and I were in the mountains
we'd read in English, French and Portuguese
without discrimination, great and small.
Too bad, I wrote a friend,
only mimosa will bloom while you're here,
nothing spectacular. "Madam-my-daughter"

was the servants' name for me; Lota
was the boss.
Who cared? I was loved
at last; an orphan at home in her citadel.
In case of emergency she'd
rush to my side to help or yell.

Then things went wrong
the way they do: job stress
(her); drinking (me).
Brazil, which once I called "hell green"
I now called hell. The phone calls,
betrayals, corruption; Latin politicians;

temperament without restraint. First she
collapsed, then me;
but she was really ill. I thought when I left
I'd be back, but she came to New York, and
killed herself
there.

My God, what a story! Too much
closure, I'd say,
if it weren't my life. Lush,

exotic settings; airplanes; death,
which casts a lying retrospective
shape. Since then two much

younger women; honors, readings,
teaching, trips. An anticlimax, then?
Perhaps. But now a piece of work
I started years ago.
Like an interminable bus ride overnight,
this poem's been a long, slow haul.

Evening falls, the destination fades.
Now all of life is in the bus;
like water trickling down
the beach, lavender and brown,
the tide long gone—
no chance of catching up, just flowing,

flowing. There'll be rhymes
shifting in their lines like fog,
slanting off each other;
people in-between things,
summing up.
Darkness and peace. When Lota died

and before, when things were really bad,
I'd add it up for friends. "We had ten years
of happiness," I'd write; or
twelve, or more, depending on my mood
and need. This poem's not like that.
I'm calling it "The Moose."

American Legions

Paris airport choked with fans
the vets celebs
one old guy watery-eyed

old, old

probably would have cried even if it weren't for lost buddies
just being back where sixty years had passed
D-Day bigger than the Academy Awards
tour buses, dawn fields crammed

Viet vets still iffy
although more consciousness now
war not their fault, Agent Orange, VA hospital scandals, etc.

Iraq vets?
Still at yellow ribbon stage
wind-tattered flags
on highway bridges
flag flag flag flag flag
white bedsheet banner, red paint:
Welcome home Danny we love you!
Highway drivers look up, feel
ironic if antiwar, sad maybe prayerful

Danny, come home . . .

Romans knew how to treat vets
Augustus, anyway.
His soldiers kicked Meliboeus out
needed his land for a vet 42 B.C.
New family relaxes in willow hedge shade

makes cheese from M's ewes' milk.
Homeless Meliboeus not envious, he says, but
"full of wonder."

Anger clearly useless, world-events-wise.
Wonder better?

Coast to Coast: Patriotism in a Time of National Disgrace

O beautiful sky this
flying day, it makes me want to wave
at their majesties,
the people of these
plains, mountains, woods beneath our wing.
My country, 'tis definitely
thee down there, on whom God shed His grace;

but God is not a *He*

it's more an amber-purple prayer for change
since these days thou
seem'st nuts. Damn! I spent my childhood
poring over place mat maps of thee!
Capitol cities in yellow, principal crops in red.
Friends talk of emigrating; I

could never go.
The seat belt sign is on again; below

unannounced, a famous place slides by
like a celebrity in street clothes or the
daylight moon. Oxbows, valleys, lakes
I *recognize*;
earth's loved crust
shoved, exploded, bunched,
watered, drained: I'm thine, thee's mine.
O window seat, o spacious day, o books I've brought along,

say, what are we to do? O ruined country,
yet I sing of thee.
If all goes well tonight I'll see

thy other shining sea.

The Tower

This poem has lain dormant many years;
in me, I mean, not Yeats. Twenty; twenty-five.
The friend I read it with is still alive.

Those were the days! We read and read.
When the couch gave out, we sat on the bed.
Why are we now estranged? I couldn't tread

the right way—*gently*—on her fears.
A woman in the poem has the ears
cut off of someone she can't stand

and brought her in a little covered dish.
Did she hate getting old, Yeats wants to know, as much as he?
Old friend, who could then foresee

how lonely, mad and wrong your life would be?
But that's Yeats's point: the "horrible splendor of desire"
and rage that shapes and spoils our lives

so no one's story makes more sense than hers
he wrote about. Reading a poem with someone else,
like sex, was something we took for granted then.

First one great work of art and then the next.
Like friends; perhaps Yeats's lady thought the same of ears:
that they'd grow back, I mean, within some years.

The years have washed this poem clean
of our old questionings. Who's Hanrahan? Where's Cloone?
Who cares? I must make sun and moonlight seem,

says Yeats, one inextricable beam.
He has: my friend's a ghost I chase across a bog
like his drowned drunk who singing lost his wits.

Blooming like paper flowers under glass
when water's added—that's my tears—
or dried-up moss or rice or anything that seems to pass

beyond the pale but comes back fresh as grass
and grief, Yeats's lines remembered me
while I forgot. Oh, fabulous Yeats's poetry,

bitter and funny as she was then,
you say we make up moonlight, ears and friends
or else they don't exist. I say that's true.

As you've made me in darkness. And I you.

Dove Cottage

How small
people were in the past and

how little
they washed! using
the bath water multiple times. They
slept sitting up, so as
not to get consumption.

How many of us
there are in this
tiny cottage; herded, nosing, curious,
like farm animals when a visitor comes
but a) we're the visitors and b) then again

how many of them
lived here
then:
the Great Man (whom we're here to catch
a glimpse of in his dirty shirt); his wife; his sister
(in his notes the letter "D")
and children (three) in this one
tiny
house.

How well the British do this kind of thing! and yet

how sick I am of tourist stress,
pervasive over-visitedness.
I'm not a poet here!
But consolation's
in a glass-cased letter that the Great Man wrote

when "neither D. nor Coleridge" liked his work.
"I have therefore been obliged," he said,
"to alter the last stanza." Now I'm fine.
I've been on either side of that one

how many times!

La Ronde

Their wives are always right about them , ex-
wives, I should say. Furious voices in emails the guy
innocently shows me, but I
totally agree with them about his
latest misdemeanor re: the kids,
sympathize with their intense frustration regarding the rowing machine
in the basement
he won't deal with.
The hollow threats, the deadlines—
I can see it all before me should I venture out onto those seas
where sturdier ships than mine have sunk.
Can you believe she talks to me like that,
he says. *No, I say, it's bad,*
and it is, I'd put it differently, but it would
amount to the same thing, i.e., *I'm so*
hurt and disappointed that I
hardly think of you as human any more
to the detriment of being particularly
human myself, get away from me, get
your act together, go, stay, fuck you.
I hear their voices,
these men's wives, saying
get already off the couch and make yourself a workspace!
or,
        stop working for once and do something with me!
Voices
        like interplanetary messages through miles and miles
of half-lit mist;
received,
although I can't reply.
Got it, thanks, I'd like to say,
if in twenty years you couldn't make that point, I guess I'll

close my mouth, move on.
But where? Some planet where
the men don't drive us nuts, then
tell us what each other said.

What's that? You ask about my ex?
Yes, I'll tell you all about it. How long

have you got?

Persephone

's life worked out, actually.
There were all the usual problems

of the hetero deal, but once
Hades cut the rough stuff

living underground was fine,
was fun. There were plenty of other

gods goddesses naiads mixed race types
part human part elf whatever

and it seemed ecological
not a punishment at all. The darkness

made everybody slow and
sensitive and into sex.

Later things deepened.
She learned what it really meant

to live beneath the dangling roots—
to live already dead—

and grew more grateful every year.
Springtimes were hard.

Getting used to the light
being with her mother again

but by summer she remembered
how much she loved it here

to Demeter's relief. Then they were
outside all day, dreaming and doing

like bees. The quiet happiness
of clouds; slow streams; fierce weeds.

From Demeter's perspective, fall struck like war
each time, and every purple aster

said, "She isn't here." Death
in her footfall, Demeter was tortured

by the wrongness of her longings;
which weren't, as one might expect,

for the days before Persephone
first left; but for those early winters

when her daughter was a victim;
raped; who longed for light

and her. Then the mother went from god to god
demanding justice.

The Use of Autobiographical Material

The reader ripping off the fig leaf of fiction
busting down the door to the house of cards
crying, *I see you!*
stamping her foot
like a crazed parent shoving receipts
in his or her kid's face
to prove there is no Santa Claus.

(The child is miles away already
walking steadily
into a deepwater silence.)

Or is the reader only

softly brushing away a diaphanous garment
which cannot really have been intended to conceal
anything but the writer's desire to be seen . . . ?

but privately, as it were;
disjunctive; to be seen in the absence of oneself
evidence found
when one has left the room

so that the reader discovers with excitement
secrets it would have bored you to read
if I'd told them to you to begin with.

Procrastination Over, I Get to Know
Some Students

One is bashful
like a woman raised in a different tradition,
some downcast, sidelong, hand-to-mouth
(to hide a smile) tradition.
Honored to be talking of Ideas,
she has dyed her hair
bright pink—wrong, wrong,
as is the eyebrow ring
on this grad-school-bound great big
girl with great
mind-mouth coordination. Another
is slender and discontent.
She stands, I sit, she, impatient, shifts
long straight black hair. A stabled
horse. *What's this class about?* she says. *Nothing real.*
What would be real is World War I
or II. I extend a carrot on a hand, which
she sniffs, but doesn't seize;
snorts, wheels, leaves.
          I am relieved
as when particularity returns
to winter days. Yesterday the snow was pock-marked.
Now great
sleet and haze.

Class

Everyone got sick—
but I mean *sick*. Plus Noah
broke his shoulder, and for days
Scott was dazed from a concussion.
Colds settled in their sinuses;
allergies erupted. I had to miss class myself
sometimes.

I couldn't tell if they liked Whitman, so I asked.
"This much?" spreading my arms; "this
much?" with just a tiny gap between my palms.
Politely they all indicated
something in
between.

Emily Dix got sick while we were doing
Emily Dickinson
which bummed out her dad as he'd named her that
on purpose.
After class I seized the book
and read Scott yet another poem.
Hadn't I worn my heart
on my sleeve enough
for one day? But after a pause,
"She's such a good writer," he deeply said.
The skin of my teeth relaxed.

Now "Thirteen Ways" by Wallace Stevens. Suddenly,
success. It's
the kind of ensemble situation I'd

fly somewhere for;
I'd get on a plane for this.
No, let me tell you
our little group taking turns today
was like Coltrane's band
on a lost great night. My lame little class.
Just Noah and Sarah and Andy
the others and me. Whoopee.

    2.

When this class ends I'll be the one
who cares, not you. And yet
in twenty years
        in ten
                in two
who'll remember who?

I'm in you, goofballs,
wait and see.

You're just a blur to me.

The Inner Game of Tennis

To slow down the ball
says the book takes
love.
      It tells some
cockamamie tale about a bull
a man enlarged by loving it.

So, *Fine!* she
chasing, swatting
thinks. *I love you!* Smack!

What's really slowed down
      truth to tell
      is his face.
From here she can read
      emotions enough for a novel but

one at a time like a gargoyle
or mask.
      Anger and pain. (Point.)
                  Resignation.
(Point.) All this she can see from the baseline,
      his face as big as a bull. *It will swell,*
said the book
        of the ball
        from love. So focus on

    the pattern of the nap;
the sound it makes when hit with string,
with wood, with gut.   Bang, and it's off

like the dog she once saw by the lake,
its owner whacking balls across the dale.
   Oh, yes, the ball's a messenger

bursting with news! Until it's not.
  At death the balls
     get closeted

   and sit there, stacked
forever, as it seems.
She'd like to use the space for clothes

but wouldn't touch this golden hoard of his—
like foreign coins or cowry shells.

I try to love that, too, she softly says,
    that fact of you
   but not so he can hear.
They've played so long
the tilted moon comes out, milky and mild
   in a still-blue sky. She tosses it
the ball and swings, but all her serves go wild.

Cheerful encouragement.
      (Point.)
        Patience.
(Point.) Now he's in despair.

Eidos, ousia, nun, stigme,

the ball coming toward her and going away,
Not his face! she says to herself,
     to the moon,
Not his face, says the moon,

     but the ball!

Archaeology

Here is the stone that we have been looking for

For years we didn't have it;
now we do

Perhaps I should look around
so I can describe how it was when they ask me.

Flat plain
white hot sky
mustard-colored earth. The detritus
of our own encampment.

There'll be
articles in the learned and popular press
a public television special

I'll tell how the diggers called me over
as usual
how it was quiet as usual—hot—

how I looked at it with perfect recognition

unremarkable as an invited friend
you don't much like.

For its part it was unmoved
beyond caring whether it was seen or left alone
time flaking off its sides like dust. No,

unlike a newborn,
full of information

the stone's a relative too old to say hello
or wonder that I've come.

This has been in the future for so long
that now it seems it happened long ago.

I cannot speak to you.

I am very hot.

Hamlet Père

May I die like Hamlet's father:
interrupted, unredeemed

in a noontime nap

from which I meant to get up and return
some badly overdue library books.

May I die with telephone numbers
of carpenters and camera stores
roaming at will among papers
I planned to round up
and label "House"
"Cat" and "Health Insurance." May I

die with friendships
in states of disrepair
and indecision, phone calls owed and intended,
catalogues marked with things

I haven't ordered yet;
having promised at least a dozen
letters of recommendation
so law schools and graduate schools up and down the East
Coast have to be notified, no, she's

dead, she won't be writing.
Let the dry cleaners call from Newton
to say, *It's June; are you ever going to come
pick up your parka?*

And my vast store of notes that might become art
can stay loose ends untied
when death stops my heart.

Poem

As I was writing it, something by Wallace Stevens
was a low gate in a picket fence,
not necessarily white. At first I thought,
don't go there,
       but had the sense to anyway.

I used a word from your dream
to describe a look on your face
       although that isn't what it means.
           Do you mind?

A whopping lie I told
can be detected if you read that poem carefully
       but only by the person I told the lie to
       and he didn't read it carefully enough.

There was a bridge from which I saw
the city and the river
every day in different weather
at a time when there was so much inner weather

I was sure that view would just
proliferate
         in words

but no. It turned out not
to be SimCity; just
a closet on a hallway
whose office doors were closed. Its silent
       open door revealed
       a stained and dripping sink.

84

A sink! I thought.
How great!—and stuck it in.

It was better by a country mile
than anything I ever planned.

Buddha Nature

What is buddha nature, asked God,
observing in a crystal ball the way moods
come and go in your mind,
historical-pastoral, allegorical-tragical
until they stop. And then there's a lull

as when the noisy launch departs,
and in the silence you can hear
the flapping of a jib. *What
is buddha nature*, asked King Lear
mid-rant;

and suddenly remembered
something else he had to do.
The theater turned to fog, to smoke, to
nothing as he left.
What is buddha nature, said the water
at slack tide when it had
time to think. It sloshed under the pier
a little, thinking
in the dark. *What*

is buddha nature, said the bird, and flew away
without the branch it had been sitting on
so much as springing back.
Stirless bird; thoughtful water; yes,
the water thought
so much about the moon
the ocean knew

exactly when to make the switch, like breath,
exactly when to quit.

What is buddha nature, said the poem
knowing when to stop.

Sabbath

A man walks out one Sabbath morn,
and sees
a fence-hole he should mend. (The man's

a rabbi, so he tries to keep the Sabbath.) He thinks
that since he even *thought* of mending it
on Saturday,
he should leave it as it was.
The unfixed fence would be

like the real white glove
the imaginary blue-frocked fairy leaves
when she flies away

or the curtains trembling still
from her departure.

It was March.
His fields were dead
his mind was gray from work

but something of the blue-gold Sabbath fluctuated
through him that next week
if he so much as thought about the hole.
But don't you think he saw another hole
the next time he walked out?
By now he'd lost a calf

so that was that. He fixed the holes.
Next month the lambs were born,
disgusting work. He had so much to do

there wasn't time to sleep—
much less to keep the Sabbath. By spring

he was one stressed rabbi,
shouting at his sons whenever they
messed up. He shouted loud enough
to drown the gorgeous May

the blossoms white and thick and
hinting heavily at something else.

Miserable, trapped, the rabbi dreamed
of crawling through some hole into
a different world—as if the world of Eastern Europe
weren't blue and gold itself that time of year.

When next he saw a hole appear,
the rabbi stopped and thought. It was a clue,

perhaps, to something: what to do or not
about Shabbat.

He stood in front of it and thought.

He could feel the Sabbath sifting
slowly
through the holes
in his understanding of it.

Safety and Danger

If a man when you kiss him
unbuttons your sweater one
shiny button at a time, does that mean Christmas
will be full of nightgowns
à la L. L. Bean? And yet when you hear those
runs and trills in unexpected places, how is that not
like a lover's here-and-there hands? . . . the melody skipping
a note; the blood rushing up
to meet the place where it wasn't. I'll

tell you where you're not. You're not
in the river any more, nor does our city, seen from above
have your name spelled out in floating
superimposed large font letters,
dayglo turquoise, perhaps, as before. My hair
tangles, something claws at it,

not you. From the bridge
an ad for online banking shows
a woman's feet in bunny slippers, something
from L. L. Bean? Okay, divorce; but
then what do I call
my ex-sister-in-law? Unlawful? It's

awful when the buzzer rips
your dream. Dreaming sex and doing it
she said, can almost be the same;
but he said no. There are lawyers in those buildings,
I've interviewed them all. From their high windows
sailboats can be seen below;
and once a steady single gull
its white wings tipped in black

was coasting, halfway up.
For seconds then I knew what cities are
and sex. That bird was legible
as text.

Custom Ring

I have dedicated the time of peak mental energy
when I could be
writing a poem
or understanding something difficult in a book

to my telephone bill. If you don't
check up on your bill
sometimes
things you

don't understand slip in
and you're
months-deep in a thicket of
local and long distance features

you didn't know existed let alone
you had, like an occult disease.
But everything starts with the telephone tree,
so you need great peace of mind.

Today I'm cool,
I don't hang up or throw the phone
but follow limb by
limb, I'm in the maze

quite possibly enclosed.
Oh the joy,
as Lewis said to Clark, when I get
word that the service representatives

are planning to take my call in its turn.
And indeed, Inez answers; but—oh no! she has
an awful voice.
How can I sort out the compulsory

Universal Connectivity Charge
from the optional Pay-Per-Use features
if she gulps and slurs
the explanation? Behind the lines

a little panic infiltrates the ranks
resulting in a little spray of
anger pellets fired by
the soldiers at the front.

Why am I doing this? Why
was I born?
Inez does a little better, I steady myself, and we
pick our way through. All goes well until I have to choose

four local features—call waiting and speed dial
aren't enough. Caller ID is the obvious choice
but I'd need a special phone. *They're*
not expensive, says Inez,

but I have a thorough intuition of what
that would mean: the trip to Best Buy,
the vast loneliness of the parking lot,
the products heavy-lidded on their shelves

my indecision, their mockery,
no, I dodge that bullet, squander my options on
useless custom ring. In the nick of time,
I realize that Inez's been

nice, really pretty nice. *Thank you,* I say.
(Glad that came out.)
It's been a pleasure doing business with you.
A slight change in her voice like the liquid call

of a finch, and we part.
I've made contact
with another human being through as it were
a wall of styrofoam peanuts. And yet

I'm very happy to be retrospectively forgiven
the $62 charge for calling abroad
when I had no International Plan; and I
definitely think the One-Rate's

right for me. I am not thinking of
my health insurance company's policy on
prescription drugs, which will have to be straightened out some day;
or the deadline for claiming the non-taxable

portion of my salary set aside to be claimed
at some later date (what date?);
or looking over a cliff
where buffalo have thundered to their death

and now lie piled. In the old king's palace
huge framed mirrors
stare in silent agony
at mirrors surrounded by

huge gilt frames
of their own. This is not that. I can have the
International Plan for a dollar
flat.

Poem Ending at the Therapist's

Free association, loose,
arisings only, spontaneity,
as when a bird and insect intersect in air
and there's
an unexpected meal.

Insects land on me,
I feel like St. Francis of Assisi
a tiny scarlet thing
one is camouflage-speckled
so funny, it leans left, pause; then
right, pause; a small striped bee
loves my pen saying "Charles Hotel," it's
lucid blue. She checks it out close up
then at a little distance, stationary, whirring.
I hold it still. You

think these line lengths are intentional? I intend,
I said, to seduce him. Your idea of an outing, he said,
is to get me into bed. Can I have
enough, can I have it till I don't want it any more, will
you stay with me? Sit there. Don't tell me we're
out of time
for now. You I can have, that's the deal.
You like it, too. You like it when
the band begins to cook. I can play you like a violin,
he said, I answered, yes,

it was all I could say. I
prefer rivers, I told you,
the Rio Reventazon, how I missed it when the outing ended
so at night I forged

across some fields until I found it,
flowing. Oh, the appeal
of flowing water, even in a lucite box, hung
up in a diner I went to with him. Little insects over

Texas Falls, golden quicknesses. I tell you these things
it begins to rain
the window streaming water, many
tiny rivers flowing down.
Here we are. A cool breeze on my bare
feet, the line lengths governed by
some principle I can't explain.
Your plant sways
a little, the closed door going back and forth
irregularly, as its tongue allows. The water streaming down the window,

an aquarium, I say, but are we the people or the fish?
Safe together here. You listen to the music wander
as if I were a violin.
This is what you want to hear.

Passenger Pigeons

1. PARIS

You return to some city you love
    and it's too exactly right

       so finding yourself again
in ever-perfect Paris
            (par exemple)
you sigh to your spouse,
      If only the kids were here.

Of course that wouldn't help.
since *even in Kyoto*
       as that slyboots, Bashō, says,
   I long for Kyoto.

Lost cities . . . worse
    losses in the natural world

flocks of rosy gold green birds
       that in my childhood, sighed John Muir,
filled the sky the livelong day
horizon to horizon—

the thought of things like these
     is hard to take. If only

I could Be There Then! Or see
        the cod
off Georges Bank that
    stayed the progress of our ship
    as an excited John

Cabot reported. Thrashing
wild excited silver fish!
You could walk on them,
some said
which I don't believe; or catch them in a basket
which I do.
That was centuries ago; but in my youth
Tim Tower said ten years ago
you could catch big sea fish here,
along the shore. *You never see that anymore,*

he said; *shaking his head*
and looking at his shoes,

never see that. That's so sad! What if we lived
when hundred-foot-high chestnut trees
were in the mountains by the millions
still? Wouldn't life be grand?
American forests! cried an ecstatic Muir.
The glory of the world!
Enough for every beast and bird and son of Man!
and nobody need have cared had there been

no pines in Norway, no cedars of Lebanon
no vine-clad selvas in the basin of the Amazon!

God help me, but that plucks my

patriotic
melancholy
strings.

2. ICE

On the 1899 expedition to
    the great ice river now known as Muir Glacier

Muir himself
    on reaching it
    got down and kissed the ice.

        Hello? Who kisses ice? As captive soldiers
    kneel and kiss the oil-stained ground
beside the landing stairs when they get home. What exile

was Muir in
        from *ice*
            that stirred him so
to see it?

        (These days,
    we should all be kissing ice, of course;

God help us all.)

3. WIND-SWEPT

Little is known of Bashō's early life
    so
two snippets
        are repeated endlessly. *At one*

time I coveted an official post with a tenure of land
is one; and

100

there was a time when I was fascinated with the ways
of homosexual love is the other. Kyoto

where I was young. I was writing then
        for fun
still expecting honor and promotion. I fucked
        whom I pleased; for fun!
Now
        in my straw hat and sandals
I sometimes pass through town

        my spirit like thin drapery
torn and swept away at the slightest stir
               of wind. Here are all the
gardens, geishas, temples that I knew; son
of a small-time samurai, I

        was having fun. Do you long
            for Kyoto, like me?

Yet there is that within me
        that one day *took to writing poetry.*
It started then as part
        of a fashionable life

but now,
        it knows no other art
            than this; and therefore
        it hangs on

            more or less blindly.

4. MONASTERY

I don't want to talk too much about Bashō
this isn't really about Bashō

but *How nice*
        he said, *just once*
NOT *to see Mt. Fuji through mist!*

And so say I! Why must we
        always peer at mountains, cities, birds, ice, fish
                through the hocus-pocus mist
of longing? Let things
just be themselves
                or not at all!

It is the people outside of the monastery
who feel its atmosphere says

Suzuki Roshi; as I was and did
        when I returned years later
        for a visit.
Tears were flowing from my eyes, nose, mouth!
And yet when I was living there,
        everyone just did what he should do.
If the wind blew through the pine trees
        it just blew.
Coming back
hearing *the bells and the monks reciting the sutra*
        I was undone. But
those who are practicing
        actually do not feel anything.

5 . SAND

Thoreau felt nothing for the still-abundant cod
in Provincetown. He wasn't moved
to see it piled *feet deep*

or set on wicker racks to dry. *Where one man*
's fish ended
         he observed, amused,
another's began—

      the villagers' yards having been *much improved*
      for this purpose. The fish, which he called
          "little treasures,"
seemed just a step

      up in value from
      the sand, something else he thought Cape Cod
had too much of. Can you believe, he said, I saw somebody
         selling it? or trying to; which proves
that a man confers a value on the most worthless thing
      by mixing himself with it. Later he

let up on sand, sounding slightly elegiac
         to find his shoes filled with *a gill* of it
      when he got home; which he used
to sand my pages with. (A gill's
      a quarter pint.) (My own ex sometimes

brought home sand in small amounts;
I found some in the basement

recently
and threw it out.) In cowhide boots

men stood atop the cod
and pitched the fish in barrows

one young dude chewing
tobacco
        and spitting. *Well, sir*, thought I,
when that older man sees you
                he will speak to you.
But presently
I saw the older man
        do the same.

6. THE WOODROW WILSON FELLOWSHIP FOUNDATION

What sets us off? Not always
what you'd think. I threw away the sand all right,
        bagged in its baggie
                with its browning twisty-tie;
but then unearthed a printed letter

well-preserved,
my name and college dormitory room
        chastely typed beneath the text.

While, it gently said, *you are not*
        obliged
                to become a college teacher,
you are expected to give

serious thought
to a career in college teaching.

That hit the spot!
      I've been a college teacher all my life! I cried.
To my surprise,
                tears were flowing from my nose, mouth and eyes!
The fatherly administrator, slightly rueful in his next
      (which brought the check)

had a mild request. *Although yours,* he said,
is not a letter-writing generation,
    still,

drop us a line sometimes
            if you can. At that I was off

like the remembered flocks of birds
the largest of them stretched
            across several States
    and belts of different kinds of weather

following the unseen leader
    never hesitating at a turn of way.

Or like a runner through the city streets
      years flying off her back like clothes
borough after borough,
        bridges, ridges, city parks.

Mine is not a letter-writing generation? *Mine?*
By the time I got back
    I was twenty again

but no one was there to greet me,
> so it felt
>> like kissing ice.
> Beneath the winter garments
>> of adulthood I had stripped to shiny runners' gear:
mesh-paneled shorts with
>> an IPodNano in their pocket
and a silky nylon-polyester shell. On my chest
pink lightning blazed
> against an ink-black skin-tight top. We used to wear

plain cotton shorts to run in; now
> *a technical fabric like CoolMax*
is thought to be a better bet
> for how it deals with sweat.
Behind the stanchions spectators were piled feet deep,
>> like cod,
> cheering and offering treats.
>>> It was
> bewildering
to be myself but young again; it is bewildering
>> this growing old.

7. GOOSE

One summer afternoon
> I chased a loon
> on Walden Pond. (The loon
is what we long for, late and soon.)
A pretty game, a man against a loon!
The loon would dive, I'd row like mad across the lake
> but it was always a mistake.

106

Straining my eyes over the water's surface one way,
     time and again
          I would suddenly be startled by his unearthly laugh
               behind me,

     says Thoreau. I don't mind chasing poems
          unexpected places; or waiting
while they dive. But now
          this one won't rise

at all; apparently the loon has died
          in the pond bottom muck
     leaving me in this
          small boat of shallow draft
marooned. Okay,

forget the loon. I'll settle for the day
an ordinary unelusive goose
     came up to me for food.

I fed her popcorn from a plastic bag;
     she loved it; so did I.
Then she tucked a leg and napped

     and the afternoon went by
me reading, her sleeping; friends;
          or at least
companions. A goose
is not a longed-for loon; but it's not a nuisance either
     as some people think.
Its shit's just grass! I saw that bird's pink
tongue in her black velvet face.

Black velvet head, immaculate
                white chinstrap
then the elegant long neck
            also black. What's wrong with that?
                Far may it be from me
to criticize Thoreau
                but even he
            eventually had
had enough. *I found,* he said as evening fell,

that it was as well for me to rest on my oars
and wait his reappearing
            as to calculate
                            where he would rise.

Surprise
            is a fundamental pleasure; so is rest.
Sometimes I remember what I read

                            and sometimes I forget.

Notes

"Donne's the One": The italicized words are from John Donne's wonderful "Holy Sonnet IV."

"Nothing Evolves, But Everything Certainly Changes": I have taken the Darwin quotation from Jonathan Weiner's *The Beak of the Finch: A Story of Evolution in Our Time.*

"Hephaestus": Hephaestus was the Greek blacksmith god, married to Aphrodite, the goddess of love. Aphrodite was more interested in Ares, the god of war. One day Hephaestus threw a net over the two of them as they made love, and all the gods stood around them and laughed.

"Conversations with the Sun": The quotations are from Carl Jung's autobiography *Memories, Dreams, Reflections.*

"The Inner Game of Tennis": The words *eidos, ousia, nun,* and *stigme* refer to forms of what philosophers have called "presence," i.e. something foundational and absolute. This particular list is from Jacques Derrida's *Of Grammatology. Eidos*: the presence of an object to sight; *ousia*: the substance or existence of something; *nun*: the exact instant of the now; *stigme*: the exact point.

"Poem": SimCity is a computer game in which the player starts from nothing and builds a whole city, complete with buildings, utilities, and so on.

"Passenger Pigeons": Tim Tower is a fisherman quoted in Carl Safina's brilliant *Song for the Blue Ocean* (Henry Holt and Company, 1997).

Acknowledgments

I am more grateful than I can say for the time, attention, material assistance and literary kinship of the following friends: Chris Bullock, Deborah Digges, Jennifer Clarvoe, Alan Feldman, Frieda Gardner, Harry George, Mark Halliday, Jonathan Haynes, Lewis Hyde, Tony Hoagland, Bob Long, Miriam Levine, Liz Mayers (*la hermana adoptiva*), Katha Pollitt, Amanda Powell, David Rivard, Laurie Sheck and Mary Watkins.

I am grateful to my excellent editor, Susan Barba, who made this process fun; and to my mother, Edythe Vigderman, for her great appreciation of my work.

In this book as elsewhere, I have depended from beginning to end on the inexhaustible talent and generosity of my sister, Patsy Vigderman. She is always on my mind as I write; and that doesn't begin to explain why I dedicate the book to her.

Earlier versions of some poems in this collection have appeared in the following places, some under different titles:

AGNI: "Donne's the One"; *BOMB*: "Yes," "Metropolitan Tang"; *Carquinez Poetry Review*: "Sound System"; *Clackamas Literary Review*: "The Tower"; *College English*: "Persephone"; *Controlled Burn*: "The Inner Game of Tennis"; *Euphony*: "Nothing Evolves (But Everything Certainly Changes)"; *Georgetown Review*: "Elizabeth Bishop on Brattle Street"; *Harvard Review*: "Sabbath," "Conversations with the Sun"; *Kenyon Review*: "Homage to Frank O'Hara"; *New Orleans Review*: "Beginning"; *Northeast Corridor*: "Whether This Marriage Is Ending: *Eyes on the Prize* and the Class of '08"; *Ploughshares*: "Academic in Traffic," "Familiarity"; *Poet Lore*: "Hairdresser Near Harvard Square"; *Raritan: A Quarterly Review*: "Crabapple," "Cormorant"; *Southern Humanities Review*: "Ecological Tourism"; *Spoon River*: "Procrastination Over, I Get to Know Some Students," "Dove Cottage"; *Westview*: "Hamlet Père"; *Wisconsin Review*: "Buddha Nature"

PHOTOGRAPH BY PETER URBAN

About the Author

LINDA BAMBER was born in Washington, D.C. and grew up both there and abroad. Having earned degrees from Vassar College, Tufts University and Columbia University, she returned to Tufts as a member of the English Department to teach literature and creative writing. Her book on Shakespeare, *Comic Women, Tragic Men* (Stanford University Press, 1992), connecting issues of gender to matters of form, has been widely excerpted and anthologized. In addition to teaching Shakespeare, she also offers courses on American poetry, Buddhism, and women writers.

Her poems, stories, essays, and reviews have appeared in *The Harvard Review, The Kenyon Review, BOMB, Tikkun, The Nation, Raritan,* and *Ploughshares,* which awarded her the Ploughshares Prize for her story, "The Time-to-Teach-Jane-Eyre-Again Blues." She lives in Cambridge, Massachusetts. *Metropolitan Tang* is her first book of poetry.